You Can
WORK IT!

Joy Berry
Illustrated by Bartholomew

Joy Berry Books
New York

Joy Berry Enterprises
146 West 29th St., Suite 11RW
New York, NY 10001

Cover Design & Art Direction: John Bellaud
Cover Illustration & Art Production: Geoff Glisson

Production Location: HX Printing, Guangzhou, China
Date of Production: July 2010
Cohort: Batch 1

Printed in China
ISBN 978-1-60577-604-0

You Can WORK IT!

Table of Contents

Self-Talk Messages

The Power of Your Mind

Your mind is extremely powerful. In fact, your thoughts affect everything that you do. If you think positive thoughts, you will most likely act in positive ways and bring positive things into your life. Conversely, if you think negative thoughts, you will most likely act in negative ways and bring negative things into your life.

Self-Talk

Self-talk is a way of communicating positive or negative thoughts to yourself. The most common forms of self-talk include thinking, talking and writing to yourself.

Thinking to Yourself

Negative Thinking:
"There is no way that I can win this competition. I wish it was over."

Positive Thinking:
"I am going to give my best effort to this competition because I want to win."

Talking to Yourself

Negative Talking:
"There is no way that I am going to do well on the test. I am not prepared."

Positive Talking:
"I am well prepared and will do well on the test. I feel confident."

Writing to Yourself

Negative Writing:
"Dear Diary, nothing has ever gone right for me and nothing is ever going to change."

Positive Writing:
"Dear Diary, although I am going through tough times, I can make things better."

Messages in Work It!

This book includes positive self-talk messages that can help you do the following:

Be Smart – Be Creative – Be Assertive – Be in Control – Get Organized – Attain Goals

There are eight self-talk messages at the end of each of the six sections of the book. By memorizing these messages and repeating them to yourself over and over again, you will begin to integrate the statements into the way that you perceive yourself and your world. And, as you do this, you will begin to think, and then act, in more positive ways. In the end, this will make you a happier, more successful person.

You Can WORK IT!

Being Smart

You can be smart if you understand
- ■ what makes a person smart,
- ■ ten guidelines for becoming a smart person,
- ■ sources of new information, and
- ■ four ways to consider the source.

Some people think that a smart person is someone who knows a lot of information.

In reality, some smart people know a lot of information. However, it is *not* this quality that makes them smart.

Some people think that a smart person is someone who has a high IQ (intelligence quotient).

In reality, some smart people have high IQs, but it is *not* this quality that makes them smart.

Some people think that a smart person is one who performs well in academic situations such as school.

In reality, some smart people perform well in academic situations. However, it is *not* this quality that makes them smart.

Many of the smartest people in the world do not know a lot of information.

Many of the smartest people in the world do not perform well in academic situations.

A smart person is one who has the ability and self-discipline to learn **relevant information.** Relevant information is information that helps a person
- survive and grow,
- accomplish necessary tasks and worthwhile goals,
- develop and maintain healthy relationships with others, and
- enjoy life.

A smart person is one who has the ability and self-discipline to put to *use* the relevant information he or she has learned.

Anyone, including you, can be a truly smart person by following several simple guidelines.

Guideline #1: Smart people determine which information is relevant and thus important for them to know. They focus their attention on learning relevant information and do not waste time learning information that is not relevant to them.

Guideline #2: Smart people realize that no one person can know everything there is to know. As a result, when they do not know something, they admit it and are not embarrassed.

Guideline #3: Smart people realize that others might know information they do not know. Therefore, they ask questions when they do not know something.

Guideline #4: Smart people listen carefully to the answers to their questions. To them it is more important to learn than to impress others with what they already know.

Guideline #5: Smart people do not automatically assume that everything they hear is true. They require substantial proof that something is true before they believe it.

Guideline #6: Smart people are not prejudiced. They do not form their opinions about something until they have carefully, with an open mind, considered *all* the information that surrounds it.

An open mind is one that is willing to believe whatever the facts reveal is true.

Guideline #7: Smart people are always re-evaluating what they think and are willing to modify their thinking if they find that it is incorrect.

Guideline #8: Smart people use their knowledge for positive rather than negative purposes.

Guideline #9: Smart people realize that their brains are crucial to intelligent thinking. Therefore, they do not do anything that would prevent their brains from functioning normally. This means that smart people
- get enough sleep,
- avoid unnecessary stress, and
- do not abuse substances (such as alcohol or drugs) that can inhibit normal brain functioning.

Guideline #10: Smart people constantly do things to keep their brains functioning creatively.

Smart people know that a healthy brain functions best when during every 24-hour period it receives approximately
- 8 to 10 hours of mental stimulation,
- 6 to 8 hours of distraction created by recreation such as playing and/or being entertained, and
- 8 hours of rest during sleep.

The brain is stimulated when it is required to put to use the information that it already knows.

The brain is also stimulated by being exposed to information that it does *not* already know.

Printed material can be a source of new information.

Television, *video,* and *radio* can also be a source of new information.

Dialogue can be a source of new information.

Lectures and demonstrations can also be a
source of new information.

Observation can be a source of new information.

Experimentation can also be a source of new information.

Most people prefer to use one or two sources of information over the others. However, no one source is better than another.

It is up to each individual to decide how he or she will gather new information.

No matter where people get their information, it is important that they *consider the source* of it.

To consider the source means to think about the context or setting in which information is given.

When smart people consider the source, they find out *who* is presenting the information and what qualifies them to do so.

Smart people disregard information from people who are not qualified to present it.

When smart people consider the source, they find out *why* the information is being presented and what the presenter hopes to accomplish.

Smart people disregard information that is presented by a person who has selfish or illogical motives for presenting the information.

When smart people consider the source, they find out the basis for the information and what proof there is that the information is valid.

Smart people disregard information that cannot be proven to be valid.

When smart people consider the source, they find out whether the information is consistent with other information that they know to be true.

Smart people disregard information that is not consistent with other information that they know to be true.

Since every person is unique and has a unique purpose in life, every person requires a unique collection of relevant information to become smart. This means that people are smart in different ways.

Smart people use relevant information to live their lives successfully. Since all people are equal, every person's collection of relevant information is important, and no one collection is more important that another. This means that no one smart person can be considered smarter than another smart person. People are merely smart in different ways.

If you want to become a smart person, you must find out what relevant information you need to know to live your life to its fullest. Then you need to intelligently use the sources that will best help you learn the relevant information you need to know.

Once you have learned information that is
relevant to you, you need to use it to
■ survive and grow,
■ accomplish necessary tasks and worthwhile
goals,
■ develop and maintain healthy relationships
with others, and
■ enjoy life.

Following the guidelines in this book will help you become a smart person.

You Can WORK IT!

Affirmations

I have the ability to learn relevant information.

I have the self-discipline to learn relevant information.

I use the relevant information I learn in a positive way.

I am a smart person.

You Can
WORK IT!

Affirmations

I keep an open mind when I am learning new information.

I consider the source of all information I receive.

I make sure the information I receive is true.

I am a smart person.

You Can WORK IT!

Being Creative

You can be creative if you know about
- the definition of creativity,
- concrete creations,
- abstract creations,
- the inherent value of creations,
- skills, talents, and gifts, and
- discovering and utilizing gifts.

To create is to bring into existence something that did not exist before.

Creativity is the ability to create. Creativity is a characteristic that is inherent in all human beings. Every person has the potential to create and, therefore, is creative.

A creation is something that has been created.

Creating is a unique process that is as important as the creation it produces. What happens to a creator while he or she is creating is as important as whatever is created.

Some creations are **concrete.**

Concrete creations are ones that are experienced with the five senses.

Some concrete creations can be looked at.

Other concrete creations can be listened to.

Some concrete creations can be tasted.

Other concrete creations can be smelled.

Some concrete creations can be touched and felt.

Other concrete creations can be useful.

Some creations are abstract.

Abstract creations are ones that can be experienced mentally and emotionally.

Some abstract creations cause people to think.

Other abstract creations cause people to experience emotions.

Some abstract creations provide a sense of
worth and well being.

Other abstract creations provide a sense of belonging.

Some abstract creations motivate people to
do things.

Other abstract creations create solutions to problems.

Some abstract creations create order.

Other abstract creations create a system or program.

Because every human being is unique, every person is uniquely creative and, therefore, produces creations that are not like any other person's creations.

Because every creation is unique, it cannot be compared to other creations to determine whether it is good or bad.

Although other people can judge a person's creation and decide whether they like it, their judgment does not make the creation good or bad.

A creator is the only person who can determine whether his or her creation is good or bad. A creator determines this by deciding whether the creation accomplishes whatever it was designed to accomplish.

Skills, talents, and gifts are used to create both concrete and abstract creations.

A skill is an ability to do something.

A skill needs to be practiced before it can be developed as well as possible.

A **talent** is a skill that a person has the potential to do very well.

Talents **cannot** be acquired. People are born with them.

A **gift** is a talent that is accompanied by an intense desire to use it.

Gifts *cannot* be aquired. People are born with them.

Every person is born with one or more gifts. Therefore, **every person is gifted.**

Important creations come into existence when people use their gifts. Therefore, people are most effectively creative when they discover and utilize their gifts.

Since gifts are accompanied by an intense desire to use them, people who do not use their gifts can become extremely frustrated and unhappy.

To avoid the frustration caused by not using a gift, it is necessary to discover and use your gifts.

You can discover your gifts by taking a **personal inventory.** To do this, make four lists.

On List #1, list the things you think you do best.

On List #2, list the things you most enjoy doing or enjoy the results of doing.

Be sure that you do not confuse enjoyment with fun. Fun is oftentimes frivolous and provides momentary pleasure. However, enjoyment provides genuine positive feelings and a sense of satisfaction that can last a long time.

On List #3, list the things you are most motivated to do. This can include things you have an intense desire to do now. It can also include things you have an intense desire to do in the future.

On List #4, list the things you do or want to do that can produce meaningful and rewarding results. This includes anything that enhances
■ your life,
■ the lives of other people, and/or
■ the world in which you live.

Once you have completed all four lists, compare them and circle those things that appear on all four lists.

The things that appear on all four lists are your gifts.

Some people have only one gift; others have more than one. How many gifts a person has is **not** what is important. What **is** important is how effectively a person uses whatever gifts he or she has.

Once you have taken a personal inventory, it is a good idea to validate your results. You can do this by talking to family members and close friends who know you well.

Before sharing the results of your inventory, ask these people to tell you what they think are your gifts. It is possible that they might come up with things you did not think of.

Next, share your personal inventory with your family members and close friends. Get their responses to your conclusions.

Evaluate their responses you get. Then decide whether you want to incorporate their responses into the process of discovering your gifts.

Another way to validate the results of your personal inventory is to talk with a professional counselor. This could be someone such as a school counselor or a career counselor.

You also can take an aptitude or career test.
These are available at
- your school,
- your community college, and/or
- a career counselor's office.

Once you have discovered your gifts, it is essential to begin developing and using them immediately.

Not developing and using your gifts can cause you to become frustrated and unhappy. This can cause you to misbehave and possibly get yourself into trouble.

Not developing and using your gifts also can rob others of the contributions your gifts were intended to produce.

This can cause others to feel resentful toward you.

Once you discover your gifts, it is imperative to find ways you can use your gifts in the future.

Then you need to do whatever is necessary to prepare yourself to use your gifts to the fullest.

People are given gifts so they can make some kind of contribution to the world in which they live.

People who do not use their gifts miss out on the opportunity to make the contributions they were born to make.

To make the most out of your life, discover and use whatever gifts you have!

You Can
WORK IT!

Affirmations

Like all human beings, I am creative.

I have a desire to create.

I have a need to create.

I create positive creations.

You Can WORK IT!

Affirmations

Like all human beings, I am gifted.

I work to discover my gifts.

I work to use my gifts.

I use my gifts to accomplish positive things.

You Can WORK IT!

Being Assertive

To say no appropriately you need to know
- the power of "no,"
- when to say no,
- when *not* to say no,
- guidelines for saying no, and
- important sayings that relate to saying no.

"No" is one of the smallest words in the English language.

Even though the word "no" is small, it is very powerful.

The word "no" can stop a person from doing something.

The word "no" can stop a person from having something.

Most people do not like to be told that they cannot do something or have something. They do not want to be told no.

Because most people do not like to be told no,
you might find that saying no is difficult.

Even though saying no might be difficult, there are times when it is necessary for you to do so.

When you are asked to do something that is wrong, you need to say no.

You need to say no when someone asks you to do something that you are not able to do.

When you are asked to do something that you do not want to do, you need to say no.

You need to say no when people offer to do something for you that you do not want them to do.

When people ask you to give them something that you do not want to give them, you need to say no.

You need to say no when someone offers you something that you do not want.

When you are asked whether you understand something that you do not understand, you need to say no.

You need to say no when someone asks whether you agree if you do not agree.

When you are asked whether you like something that you do not like, you need to say no.

You need to say no when you are asked whether you feel the way someone else thinks you should feel if you do not feel that way.

When you are asked to be with someone you don't want to be with, you need to say no.

There are times when you should say no. There are also times when you should *not* say no.

Do not say no when you are asked to stop doing something that will hurt you or another person.

Do not say no when someone asks you to do something for your safety or the safety of others.

Do not say no when you are asked to do
something that you are supposed to do.

Do not say no when saying no is a lie.

If and when you need to say no, you need to do it appropriately. You can accomplish this by following six guidelines.

Guideline One. Get the facts.

Find out exactly what the question is.

Find out what will happen if you say yes and if you say no.

Also find out exactly what you will be expected to do if you say yes and if you say no.

Guideline Two. Think about it.

Think about how your decision might affect you
or others.

Ask yourself, "How will my decision affect me and other people? Will it be helpful or harmful?"

Remember that it is important to avoid making any decision that could harm you or other people.

Guideline Three. Answer the question as soon as possible.

Once you know the answer to a question, tell your answer to the person who asked the question.

Do not make the person wait any longer than necessary.

Do not let anyone believe you are going to say yes when you are going to say no.

And do not let anyone believe you are going to say no when you are going to say yes.

Guideline Four. Be clear.

Some people might avoid saying the word "no" by:

- pretending that they were not asked the question,
- refusing to give an answer to the question,
- getting upset because they were asked the question, or
- giving all the reasons they want to say no without actually saying no.

Because these actions can be misunderstood, they should not be used to communicate the word "no."

If your answer to a question is no, you need to say it. Saying the word "no" is the only way people can be absolutely sure that you mean no.

Guideline Five: Be reasonable.

If you have good reasons for saying no, it is good to share them with the other person. This might help the person understand why you are saying no and help him or her accept your answer.

Sometimes you might not know the reasons for your decision, or you might not want to share them with anyone. In either situation, you do not have to give your reasons.

Give your reasons only if you know exactly what they are, or if it will be helpful to you or others to share them.

Guideline Six. Be kind.

It is important to be kind when you tell a person no.

You can be kind by speaking kindly. Avoid talking loudly and avoid saying mean things.

You can also be kind by adding some kind words to your "no" answer.

Here are three examples of kind words you can add.

Example #1: "No, thank you."

Example #2: "No, maybe some other time."

Example #3: "I'm sorry, but no."

There are several important sayings that relate to saying no.

First saying: "Never say 'no' if you can possibly say 'yes.' "

This means that because you often make others happy when you say yes, you should say it whenever possible.

Second saying: "Let your 'yes' be 'yes' and your 'no' be 'no.'"

This means that you should do your best to stay with any decision you make. Try not to change your mind too often, since this can confuse and frustrate you as well as the people around you.

Third saying: "There is no law against changing your mind."

This means that it is OK for you to occasionally change your mind. If you discover new facts or have new feelings that prove you made a wrong decision, you should change your decision. However, if you need to change your decision, it is important for you to think carefully so that your new decision will be correct.

Fourth saying: "You can please some of the people all of the time and all of the people some of the time, but you can't please all of the people all of the time."

This means that it is impossible to make everyone happy all of the time. Therefore, you should not feel bad when, on occasion, another person is disappointed by a decision you make.

Fifth saying: "Turnabout is fair play."

This means that if you have a right to do something, other people have the right to do the same thing. If you have a right to say no, other people have a right to say no, too.

If you expect other people to respond in a positive way when you say no, you need to respond in a positive way when they say no.

If you say no appropriately, you will be doing the right thing for you and the people around you.

You Can
WORK IT!

Affirmations

I have the right to be honest.

I have the right to say "no."

I respect and encourage the right of others to be honest.

I respect and encourage the right of others to say "no."

You Can WORK IT!

Affirmations

I realize that "no" is a positive word.

I say "no" only after careful thought and consideration.

I am reasonable and kind whenever I say "no."

I say "no" only when it is necessary for me to do so.

You Can
WORK IT!

Being In Control

You can become your own boss by learning about

- control and responsibility,
- three ways to accept responsibility for your life,
- how to determine whether you are a responsible person, and
- things that keep you from being responsible.

If you are like most people, you would like to have complete control over your life. You would like to decide
■ whom you are going to be with,
■ what you are going to do,
■ when you are going to do things, and
■ where you are going to go.

If you are like most people your age, you do not have complete control of your life.

You have not had complete control over your life because you have not been completely responsible for it. Other people, such as your parents or guardians, have been responsible for keeping you alive. It has been their job to provide you with everything you need to survive and grow.

Your parents or guardians have also been responsible for keeping you safe. It has been their job to protect you from anything that might hurt you. It has also been their job to keep you from hurting yourself.

Your parents or guardians have been responsible for keeping you from hurting other people.

It has also been their job to make sure that you do not damage or destroy other people's property.

Your parents or guardians could not have
protected and provided for you without
controlling you. If they did not control you, they
could not have kept you from harming yourself
or others.

Therefore, other people have controlled your life because they have been responsible for it.

The only way you can have more control over your life is to accept more responsibility for it. There are three ways in which you can accept more responsibility for your life.

One way is to **be responsible for yourself.** Do whatever you need to do to keep yourself well.

Do whatever you need to do to keep yourself safe.

Handle your emotions in a way that will benefit you and others.

Solve your problems and make your decisions intelligently.

Develop your skills, abilities, and talent. Use them in a positive way.

Learn everything you need to know to grow and become a better person.

A second way to become more responsible for your life is to **be responsible for your relationships with others.** In other words, treat other people the way you want to be treated. Do not do anything that would hurt another person.

Do not do anything that would damage or
destroy another person's property.

Communicate with other people kindly and honestly.

Be fair. Do not take more than you give. If people give you something, make sure you give them something in return.

Be truly sorry when you have done something to hurt another person. Apologize and ask the person to forgive you. Then, do whatever you can to make the other person feel better.

Forgive other people when they have done something to hurt you.

A third way to become responsible for your life is to **be responsible in the way you use things.** Learn as much as you can about the things you use so that you can use them appropriately.

Do not abuse the things you use.

Do not use anything in a way that could hurt you.

Do not use anything in a way that could hurt other people.

You will be a responsible person if you are
■ responsible for yourself,
■ responsible in relationships with others, and
■ responsible in the way you use things.

If you are a responsible person, you will have more control over your life.

There are several ways to determine whether you are a responsible person.

You are a responsible person if you **think for yourself.** This means that you make your own evaluations. Before you do something, you consider whether it is the right or wrong thing to do. You ask yourself, "Will what I am about to do have a positive or negative effect on me or others?" If the answer to your question is, "It will have a positive effect," you know that it is the right thing to do. If the answer is, "It will have a negative effect," you know that it is the wrong thing to do.

You are a responsible person if you **have self-control.** This means that no one, other than yourself, has to keep you from doing something that is wrong. No one has to tell you not to do something. No one has to bribe you or threaten to punish you. You avoid doing something that is wrong because you know it is wrong and you choose not to do it.

You are a responsible person if you are **self-motivated.** This means that no one, other than yourself, has to make you do something that needs to be done. No one has to tell you to do something. No one has to bribe you or threaten to punish you. You do what needs to be done without depending on others to get you started or keep you going.

You are a responsible person if you **are dependable.** This means that you can be trusted. You keep any promise you make to yourself or others. You do exactly what you say you are going to do.

You are a responsible person if you **are conscientious.** This means that you give your very best effort to whatever you attempt to do. You do the best job you can do, no matter how large or small the task is.

You are a responsible person if you **are honest with yourself.** This means that you do not blame others for your mistakes or misbehavior. When you make a mistake or do something wrong, you realize that it is your fault, and you admit it. You apologize and do whatever you can to correct the situation.

There are several things that can keep you from becoming a responsible person.

Feeling Inadequate

You might feel inadequate. You might feel that you are not capable enough to be responsible. You might think that you cannot do the things you need to do to be a responsible person.

If you feel inadequate, you need to remember this: When you were born, you were given a life to live. You were also given everything you need to live that life. You have within you all the intelligence and ability you need to live your life to the fullest. No one can live your life better than you can.

Being Afraid to Fail

You might be afraid to fail. You might be afraid that if you take responsibility for your life, you will fail and ruin your life.

If you are afraid to fail, you need to remember this: Failure does not have to ruin your life. In fact, failure can be beneficial. It can give you an opportunity to learn what you should and should not do. If you fail because you did something wrong, you can learn to avoid doing the same thing again. If you fail because you neglected to do something, you can learn to do it next time. Therefore, you should not be afraid to fail because failure can teach you valuable lessons.

Wanting to Blame Others

You might want other people to be responsible for your life so that you can blame them when things go wrong. You might think that if other people are to blame when things go wrong, they will have to make things right.

If you want to blame others when things go wrong, you need to remember this: It is your job to live your life. When something goes wrong with your life, it does not matter whose fault it is. It is your job to make it right. No one can do this for you.

Wanting To Be Lazy

Being lazy can keep you from becoming a responsible person. You might think that it is too much work to be responsible. You might not want to spend the time and make the effort it takes to be a responsible person.

If you feel like being lazy, you need to remember this: Whether you or someone else is responsible for your life, living it fully takes time and effort. Whether you or someone else makes your decisions, you are going to have to respond by doing something. No matter how much another person helps you, there is no way to completely avoid putting time and effort into your own life.

The amount of control you have in your life depends on the amount of responsibility you assume. This means that the less responsibility you accept for your life, the less control you will have over it.

The more responsibility you accept for your life, the more control you will have over it.

Growing up means assuming more and more responsibility for your life. It means becoming a responsible person. When you become a responsible person, you will become your own boss!

You Can
WORK IT!

Affirmations

I assume responsibility for myself.

I assume responsibility in my
relationships with other people.

I am responsible in the way that I relate
to the things in my environment.

Because I am responsible, I am
in control.

You Can WORK IT!

Affirmations

I think for myself.

I have self contol and am self motivated.

I am honest, conscientious and dependable.

I am a responsible person and I am in control of my life.

You Can WORK IT!

Getting Organized

You can get organized by learning
- the difference between being organized and disorganized,
- how to organize your possessions,
- how to organize your space, and
- how to organize your time.

You are **organized** when the space in which you function is neat and orderly. You are also **organized** when your possessions are where they belong.

You are **organized** when you are doing the right things in the right place at the right time.

You are **disorganized** when your belongings are out of place.

You are disorganized when the space in which you function is messy and disorderly.

You are **disorganized** when you are doing the wrong things in the wrong place at the wrong time.

Being disorganized can cause you to become confused and frustrated. It can keep you from doing the things you need and want to do.

If you are disorganized, you can cause the people around you to become confused and frustrated. Their confusion and frustration might cause them to become angry at you.

Being organized can make life simpler and more pleasant for you and the people around you.

To be organized, you must efficiently manage your
▪ possessions,
▪ space, and
▪ time.

To organize your possessions, you need to follow six steps.

Step One: Get four large boxes and label them.

Label the first box "Toss."
Label the second box "Recycle."
Label the third box "Hold."
Label the fourth box "Use."

Step Two: Put your possessions in a pile.

Step Three: Sort your possessions into the four boxes.

Pick up one possession at a time and put it in one of the four boxes. Do not put the item back in the pile.

All of the possessions that are no longer useful should be put in the box marked "Toss."

Usable possessions you do not want any more should be put in the box marked "Recycle."

When you have not used something for a long time and are not sure you want to get rid of it, put it in the box marked "Hold."

All the possessions you want to keep and use
should be put in the box marked "Use."

Step Four: Distribute the four boxes.

Put the contents from the box marked "Toss" in the trash.

Get rid of the possessions in the "Recycle" box.
The items in this box can be
- given to a friend,
- traded for something else,
- sold, or
- given to an organization that recycles used
  things.

Close up the "Hold" box. Write the date on it. Then store the box in a safe place.

If a year goes by and you have not missed the possessions in your "Hold" box, you probably don't need them. In this case, put the unwanted items in the "Recycle" box the next time you organize your possessions.

Step Five: Sort the possessions in the box marked "Use."

The items in this box can most likely be divided into these groups:

1. Reading material (such as books, magazines, and comic books)
2. School materials (such as notebooks and homework)
3. Arts and crafts materials
4. Stationery supplies (such as paper, pencils, and erasers)
5. Hobbies (such as model airplanes and miniatures)
6. Collections (such as stamps, rocks, and baseball cards)
7. Toys and games
8. Equipment (for sports, bikes, etc.)
9. Music and musical instruments
10. Clothing (including shoes and boots)
11. Personal supplies (such as combs, brushes, and perfume)
12. Mementos (such as photographs, scrapbooks, and keepsakes)

Step Six: Put away the items from the "Use" box.

- Put anything smaller than a Ping-Pong ball into plastic storage bags. This includes items such as game parts, accessories, and model pieces.
- Place items the size of a baseball in shoe boxes or covered cans.
- Store all the items in one group together in a box if there is no room in drawers or closets.
- Label your possessions so they can be returned to you if they are misplaced.
- Label drawers, shelves, and boxes so anyone who puts away your things will put them in the right place.
- Get rid of worn-out or outgrown things before you put away any new ones so you won't have to dig through the pile of old things to get to the new ones.

Here are a few tips for organizing your clothes:

■ Group your clothes according to a plan. You might want to put all your shirts or blouses together, all your pants together, and so on. Or you might want to put your play clothes together and your good clothes together. Any plan you decide to use should help you find things more easily.

■ Put freshly laundered clothes on the bottom of the stacks of folded clothes in your drawers and on your closet shelves. Use the clothes on the top first. If you do this, everything will be worn, and you won't end up wearing the same clothing over and over.

It will be easier for you to organize your possessions if you **work in a clean area.**

It will also help if you work with **one group of possessions at a time**.

Your space includes the areas you live in and use. At home it might be your bedroom and bathroom. At school it might be your desk or locker. To organize your space, you need to follow four rules:

Rule One: Every item in your space should have a purpose.

Every item in your space should have a reason for being there. Get rid of items that do not have a purpose. Useless items take up valuable space and make it difficult to keep the area organized.

Rule Two: Every item in your space should be used properly.

You should use every item in the way it was intended to be used. For example, a clothes hamper, rather than a chair, should be used to collect dirty clothes. A trash can, rather than a drawer, should be used to collect trash. Beds should be used for resting, not for hiding junk. Rugs should be used to cover the floor, not to cover dirt.

Rule Three: Every item in your space should be assigned to a specific place.

Every item in your space should have a certain place where it can be stored. If there is not a specific place for something, you need to create a place for it. To do this, you can

- get rid of something you do not use,
- use boxes or other containers for storage, or
- make a shelf by stacking a board on some cinder blocks or bricks.

Rule Four: Every item in your space should be in its place when it is not used.

When you have finished using something, you should carefully put it back in its place. If you do this, your possessions will not become damaged and your space will look neat and orderly.

It will be easier for you to put things away if you store them properly.

Things used often should be put in places that are easy to reach.

Things used occasionally can be stored in places that are not so easy to reach.

To organize the time you spend doing various activities during the day, you need to follow four steps.

Step One: Gather together the necessary equipment and supplies.

You will need
- a clock (preferably an alarm clock),
- a watch (optional),
- a wall or desk calendar (with space in which to write),
- a date book,
- a note pad, and
- a sharpened pencil.

Here's what to do:

- Put the clock in a place where you can easily see and use it. If you have a watch, wear it.
- Hang the calendar or put it in a place where you can easily see it and use it.
- Carry the date book with you or keep it at school.
- Keep the note pad by your calendar.
- Keep a sharpened pencil by the calendar and note pad.

Step Two: Gather together dates and information.

Go to the office at your school. Get the dates for
- school vacations,
- school holidays, and
- school events.

If you belong to a team, club, or organization, talk to the people in charge. Get the information for
■ regular meetings (such as practices and weekly get-togethers) and
■ special meetings (such as games and parties).

Be sure to get the date, time, and location of each event.

Talk to your parents or guardians. Get the information for
- family vacations,
- family holidays, and
- family activities (such as parties and outings).

Be sure to get the date, time, and location of each event.

Write the information you have gathered on your calendar and in your date book. Write the name, time, and location of each event next to its scheduled date.

Use a pencil when you write so you can erase the information if your plans change. This will help you avoid making a mess of your calendar or your date book.

Step Three: Maintain your calendar.

When someone asks you to do something, check your calendar or date book. Look at the date and time he or she has asked you about. If nothing is written for that time, you can think about doing what the person has asked you to do.

If you decide to do what someone has asked you to do, write the information about the event on your calendar and in your date book.

Check your calendar at the beginning of each day to remind yourself of activities planned for the day. Mark off each day or event on your calendar after it occurs.

Step Four: Maintain a things-to-do list.

Anytime you think of something that needs to be done, write it on the note pad next to your calendar. If you are not near your note pad, write a message about the task on a scrap of paper. Put the message in your pocket or purse. When you get to your note pad, transfer the message from the scrap of paper to the note pad. Be sure to check your pockets or purse for your messages at the end of each day.

Check your note pad at the beginning of each day. Decide when and how you are going to do tasks listed on the note pad. As much as possible, do what you have decided to do during the day.

At the end of every day, check your note pad.
Cross off the things you have done.

Put the things you have not done at the top of your list for the next day.

There are two sayings that might help you as you go over your things-to-do list.

First saying: "First things first."

You need to do the most important things on your list first. The other things should be done in order of their importance.

Second saying: "One step at a time."

You might feel overwhelmed if you try to do everything at the same time. When you have a lot of things to do, you need to do them one at a time.

Life is easier and more pleasant for you and the people around you when you organize your
■ possessions,
■ space, and
■ time.

You Can
WORK IT!

Affirmations

Organization can eliminate the confusion and frustration in my life.

Organization can create order and enhance my productivity.

Organization can help me do the things I need and want to do.

My need and desire for organization make getting organized a wonderful experience for me.

You Can WORK IT!

Affirmations

I have the energy and the ability to get organized.

The time and effort I put into getting organized is worthwhile.

I will do whatever is necessary to get organized.

I will carefully and consistently maintain the organization that I have created.

You Can
WORK IT!

Attaining Goals

You can get what you want if you understand
- desires and goals,
- four steps to achieving goals,
- eight obstacles to achieving goals,
- ten qualities of acheivers, and
- how to become an achiever.

If you are like most people, you have **desires.** Your desires are the things you would like to be, do, or have.

If you desire things enough to do whatever
is necessary to get them, your desires become
goals.

A goal is something a person wants and tries
to achieve.

There are two basic kinds of goals.

Short-term goals usually require a minimum amount of effort and can be achieved in a short time.

Long-term goals usually require more effort and can be achieved only over a longer period of time.

Sometimes it is necessary to achieve several short-term goals in order to achieve a long-term goal.

Usually, the effort and time invested in achieving a goal are proportionate to the benefits derived from achieving the goal. The greater the investment of effort and time, the greater the reward.

You can achieve any goal as long as you are **able and willing** to make it happen.

To achieve a goal you must be physically and mentally capable of achieving it.

To achieve a goal you must be willing to do whatever is necessary to make it happen.

Achieving a goal is easier when you follow four basic steps.

Step 1: Define the goal.

Establish exactly what is your goal. Avoid general goals such as "I want to be happy" or "I want to be successful." Instead, try to be specific.

Specific goals represent particular accomplishments. For example, learning how to do a particular task or acquiring something in particular is a specific goal.

Having specific goals makes it easier to determine exactly what needs to be done to achieve them.

Step 2: Make a list.

List the tasks that need to be done to achieve the goal.

It might be beneficial to have someone help you make the list.

Talk to a person who is experienced in setting and achieving goals.

Or, talk to a person who has achieved a goal that is similar to yours.

Step 3: Organize the list.

List the tasks in order of how they need to be accomplished. List what needs to be done first, second, third, and so on.

It might be helpful to list each task on a small slip of paper. Place the slips on a flat surface. Organize them in a vertical row with the first task at the top of the row and the last task at the bottom.

Copy the list of tasks in proper order onto a sheet of paper. This will become a "Things to Do" list.

Step 4: Do each task.

Work from the "Things to Do" list and do whatever needs to be done to achieve the goal.

Start from the top of the list and complete each task in order.

When you complete a task, cross it off your list and move on to the next task.

Keep going until you have crossed off every task on the list. At this point you will have achieved your goal.

Sometimes you might not want to do a task on the "Things to Do" list. However, to achieve your goal, sometimes it is necessary to do things you might not want to do.

Avoid procrastinating.

Do not put off doing a job. Do it as soon as possible.

Avoid escaping.

Do not try to get out of doing a task by doing something else. Focus your attention on the task that needs to be done and stick with the job until it is finished.

Here are some things you can do to make an undesirable task easier to accomplish.

Race with the clock.

Set a time limit for the task. Then try to get the job done in the allotted time or sooner.

Reward yourself.

Promise yourself you will do something you truly enjoy after you finish a task. Then keep the promise you make to yourself.

Here are several obstacles that can make achieving your goals difficult. It is important for you to overcome these obstacles if you are to get what you want.

Obstacle 1. Negative people

Some people might not believe you are capable of achieving your goals. Others might think your goals are impossible to achieve. People who have these negative thoughts can influence you to think as they do. This can damage your self-confidence and make it difficult for you to achieve your goals.

It is important for you to avoid being around people who have negative thoughts about you and your goals.

Obstacle 2. Nonsupportive people

Some people who have less than you might be critical or jealous of you. This can make you feel bad.

Some people who have more than you might be judgmental and feel superior to you. This can make you feel bad.

Bad feelings can keep you from achieving your goals.

You need to develop worthwhile values. Then you need to develop relationships with people who support those values.

Obstacle 3. Worry

It takes time to worry. It also takes physical, mental, and emotional energy. In spite of this, worrying seldom accomplishes anything positive. It only upsets you and keeps you from achieving your goals.

The time and energy you use worrying are not used to do what you need to do. Therefore, you should not waste your time or energy worrying. Instead, focus on achieving your goals.

Obstacle 4. Indecision

Deciding what to do is the first step toward achieving a goal. If you do not take this first step, you cannot take the other necessary steps and the result will be doing nothing at all.

You might be indecisive because you are afraid you will make the wrong decision and fail. However, in most cases the most effective way to know whether a decision is right or wrong is to act on it.

You might need to try many things before you reach the right decision.

Obstacle 5. Laziness

Achieving a goal takes work. Many people do not want to work. They are lazy.

Laziness can turn you into a passive person who *waits* for things to happen instead of an active person who *causes* things to happen. Laziness might make you pass up an opportunity to get what you want if that opportunity requires some effort.

If you want to achieve your goals, you must take advantage of every opportunity that comes your way. You must be willing to work.

Obstacle 6. Overdependence on others

Many people do not want to work to achieve their goals. They would rather depend on someone else to do or get things for them.

Depending on others can be frustrating because you have no control over them. You cannot be sure they will come through for you.

The only person over whom you have complete control is yourself. If you learn to work to get the things you want, you will not be completely dependent on others and you will gain more control over your own situation.

Obstacle 7. Mistreating others

It will be impossible for you to accomplish all of your goals all by yourself. Sometimes you will need other people to help you. People will be more willing to help you if you are honest and fair.

To be sure that you are honest and fair, you need to treat other people the way you want to be treated.

Obstacle 8. Dissatisfaction

Achieving goals will not make you happy unless you learn to appreciate what you have. You will not be happy if all of your thoughts are focused on the things you do not have. You will not be happy if you are always feeling that you do not have enough.

You must focus on what you *do* have, rather than what you *do not* have. This will help you enjoy your achievements and will make you feel that your efforts are worthwhile.

If you achieve your goals, you will become an achiever. Achievers are people who reach their goals. Achievers share many positive qualities.

Quality #1 — Motivation

Achievers have a strong desire to achieve their goals.

Quality #2 — Confidence

Achievers believe in themselves. They realize they have the potential to achieve many things. They believe they can do almost anything they decide to do.

Quality #3 — Open-mindedness

Achievers are willing to listen to others and learn from them. Before they do anything, they consider the advice they get from trustworthy people.

Quality #4 — Flexibility

Achievers are willing to change when they find a way to improve. They are also willing to change their plans when they discover a better way to accomplish their goals.

Quality #5 — Courage

Achievers are willing to take a chance. They make an effort to achieve their goals, even though they might fail or be criticized by others.

Quality #6 — Initiative

Achievers are ambitious. They never put off what needs to be done. They do every task as soon as possible.

Achievers work independently. They try not to depend on others to get them started or keep them going.

Quality #7 — Conscientiousness

Achievers are conscientious. They give their
very best effort to whatever they attempt to do.
No matter how large or how small the task,
they do the best job they can do.

Quality #8 — Discipline

Achievers are willing to give up something
they enjoy if it could keep them from achieving
their goals.

They are also willing to do things they might
not want to do if it will help them achieve
their goals.

Quality #9 — Concentration

Achievers do not allow things to distract them or keep them from doing what they need to do.

They focus their attention and efforts on achieving their goals.

Quality #10 — Perseverance

Achievers keep going. If what they are doing is right, they never give up.

You can achieve your goals if you
■ are able and willing,
■ follow the four steps to achieving goals,
■ overcome the eight obstacles that might keep
   you from achieving your goals, and
■ nurture the ten qualities that will make you
   an achiever.

People who achieve very few goals are called underachievers.

People who do not achieve goals are called nonachievers.

People are not *born* achievers, underachievers, or nonachievers.

People *become* achievers, underachievers, or nonachievers.

You can become an achiever if you choose to be one *and* do whatever is necessary to achieve your goals. This means that getting what you want is up to you!

You Can
WORK IT!

Affirmations

I define my goals.

I list the tasks that are necessary to achieve my goals.

I set priorities for the tasks that are on my list.

I accomplish the tasks in the order of their priority.

You Can
WORK IT!

I overcome any obstacle that might prevent me from achieving my goals.

I develop the qualities that can help me achieve my goals.

I do whatever is required to achieve my goals.

I get what I want.